Baby Purees

This edition published by Parragon Books Ltd in 2013
and distributed by

Parragon Inc.
440 Park Avenue South, 13th Floor
New York, NY 10016
www.parragon.com

Copyright © Parragon Books Ltd 2013

Illustrated by Annabelle Ozanne
Designed by Amy Child

ISBN 978-1-4723-2387-3

Printed in China

Contents

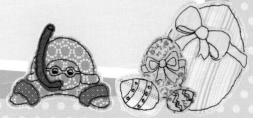

Introduction

Weaning is an important milestone in your baby's development and an exciting time for both you and your little one. Good nutrition is essential for healthy growth and development and what a child eats in infancy and childhood can have a lasting effect on their health. As a parent, you play an important role in teaching your child to enjoy a wide range of foods and helping to establish good eating habits for life.

Whether you choose to use homemade or store-bought baby foods depends entirely on your personal preference and circumstances—many parents use a combination of both. Commercial baby foods can certainly be convenient, especially when traveling, so it's useful to have a few jars or packages in the pantry. However, contrary to popular belief, preparing your baby's food yourself doesn't have to take a lot of time or be a major effort, especially if you cook in batches and freeze the leftovers for another day. It also offers a number of advantages.

First, and perhaps top of the list, is the fact that you have full control over everything your baby eats—you will know exactly what has gone into their food and can ensure that it is fresh, nutritious, and free from any additives. You can also introduce a greater variety of food into your baby's diet than if you were relying on the flavors and ingredients chosen by manufacturers (for example, you're unlikely to find fruit and vegetables like melons, zucchini, or avocados in many commercial baby foods).

Making your own baby purees is also a very economical way of feeding your baby—something that cost-conscious families are sure to appreciate! It is also the best way to get them used to eating family food when they are older, because the tastes and textures will be familiar.

WEANING YOUR BABY

Weaning is the gradual process that begins when you start to introduce solid foods into your baby's diet. At around the age of six months, milk alone cannot satisfy all your baby's nutritional needs. Their stores of nutrients, such as iron, start to run out and need to be supplemented by a more varied diet. Moving on to more solid foods also helps to develop the muscles necessary for chewing and, eventually, for speech.

The American Academy of Pediatrics recommends breast-feeding as the sole source of nutrition for babies for the first six months of life, but the exact age to start giving solids depends entirely on the individual baby. Every baby is different and what suits one baby isn't necessarily right for another. There is no advantage in weaning a baby earlier than necessary. In fact, there are several good reasons why the early introduction of solids is not a good idea. Before the age of four months, your baby's digestive system may not have developed enough to cope with foods other than breast or formula milk. Early weaning may also increase the risk of food allergy because the digestive system is not yet fully developed at this age.

HOW WILL YOU KNOW WHEN THE TIME IS RIGHT?

When a baby has doubled their birth weight or reached 13 pounds, it's a good time to start looking for signs that they may be ready to be weaned. If your baby still seems hungry after a good milk feed, or wants to feed more frequently than usual, it is often a sign that they are ready for solids. If you are in any doubt, discuss the matter with your healthcare professional.

During the early stages of weaning, purees are given in addition to the normal quantity of breast or bottle feeds, but as your baby starts to eat larger amounts you can gradually cut down on the milk feeds. However, your baby will continue to need to drink 2 cups a day of breast milk, infant formula, follow-on milk (from six months) or cow's milk (from 12 months) until around the age of five.

FOODS TO AVOID

• You should never add **salt** to foods for babies. Even if the food tastes bland to you, it will be fine for your baby. Do not use **bouillon cubes** or **gravy mix** as they can be high in salt. Check the sodium/salt content on ready-made foods—babies under 12 months should consume less than a gram of salt per day.

• Avoid canned foods that contain **added sugar** or **added salt**. Use canned corn or beans in water, and canned fruit in natural juice instead of syrup. Canned fish, such as tuna, should be packed in spring water or oil.

• Don't add **sugar** or **sweeteners** to your baby's food. Adding sugar can encourage a sweet tooth and lead to tooth decay. Sweeteners, such as agave syrup, brown sugar, honey, evaporated cane juice, or fructose, are no healthier than sugar. Babies should not be given **honey** until they are at least 12 months old because it can contain a type of bacteria that can cause serious illness.

• Foods containing **gluten** (including bread, pasta, and some breakfast cereals) should not be introduced until after the age of six months.

• Children under five should not be given **whole nuts** as they may cause choking. Nut butters and crushed or ground nuts are okay.

• **Unpasteurized milk** and **cheeses** are not suitable for the under-ones.

• **Low-fat foods** are not suitable for babies and children under the age of two because fat is an important source of calories and some vitamins.

• **Raw and lightly cooked eggs** should he avoided. Eggs can be given to babies over six months, but make sure they are thoroughly cooked until both the white and yolk are solid.

• Babies should not be given **shark**, **swordfish**, or **marlin**. This is because the relatively high levels of mercury in these fish can affect a baby's growing nervous system.

• **Raw meat**, **fish**, and **shellfish** should not be given to children under the age of 5 years because of an increased risk of food poisoning.

• **Liver** should be limited to one small serving a week because of high levels of vitamin A.

FOOD SAFETY

Good food hygiene is important for everyone but when you are preparing and cooking food for babies it is obviously more important than ever.

• Before you start preparing food, always wash your hands thoroughly with hot water and an antibacterial hand wash, then dry them with a clean towel.

• Make sure all your equipment is as clean as possible. If you have decided to wean your baby before they are six months old, all equipment should be sterilized. Once your baby is 6 months old, there is no need to sterilize their bowls and cutlery. If you have a dishwasher, all equipment should be placed on the top shelf and washed using the highest temperature setting (but check it is dishwasher-proof first). If you are washing by hand, use hot, soapy water.

• Always wash your hands in between touching raw and cooked foods. Use separate knives, cutting boards, and utensils for preparing raw and cooked foods, or wash them thoroughly in hot, soapy water.

• Store raw and cooked foods on separate shelves in the refrigerator, making sure that any raw foods cannot drip onto cooked foods.

• If you are preparing food to be frozen, freeze it as soon as possible after cooking but never put hot food straight into the refrigerator or freezer. If you are cooking a large quantity of food to freeze, it will cool much quicker if it is divided into smaller portions, or transferred into a container with a large surface area. During warm weather, place the container into a bowl of ice water. Food should be cooled and refrigerated within one hour of being cooked.

• Never refreeze food that has been frozen previously, unless it has been cooked in between (e.g. If a frozen raw meat, such as beef mince, is defrosted and cooked to make something like a Bolognese sauce, the dish can be refrozen).

• If you are using a jar or bottle of baby food, use a clean spoon to transfer the amount you need to a small bowl. Throw away any food that your baby doesn't eat—do not return it to the container.

• Heat food thoroughly and allow it to cool before feeding it to your baby. Heat homemade food in a microwave or in a saucepan on the stove until it is piping hot. Stir the food well and test the temperature before offering it to your baby (this is especially important if you used a microwave to heat it). If you are using jars of baby food, stand them in a saucepan of hot water to heat them up. Never reheat food more than once, and throw away any leftovers.

Banana Yogurt

Bananas, when they are well ripened, are easy for your baby to digest and can be mashed into a smooth paste. This dessert is the perfect way to introduce yogurt into your child's diet.

INGREDIENTS:

½ small ripe banana

a few drops of vanilla flavoring

2-3 tablespoons Greek-style yogurt

PREPARE
5 minutes

COOK
0 minutes

SERVINGS
1

1. Peel the banana and mash with a fork until smooth.

2. Stir the vanilla flavoring into the banana puree, then layer with the yogurt in a small serving bowl.

3. Serve immediately. Do not refrigerate or freeze.

Apple and Pear Puree

Apples and pears are closely related and blend well together. In common with bananas and fruits with pits, they are considered to be low-allergenic, so are particularly suitable as first fruits for young children.

INGREDIENTS:

- 1 McIntosh, Fuji, or Pippin apple
- 1 ripe Bosc pear
- 3 tablespoons water

PREPARE
5 minutes

COOK
7–10 minutes

SERVINGS
4–6

1. Peel, core, and dice the apple and pear. Put all the ingredients into a saucepan and bring to a boil. Reduce the heat, cover, and simmer for about 7–10 minutes, until very soft. Check regularly to make sure that the fruit has not caught on the bottom of the saucepan. Leave to cool a little.

2. Drain the fruit, reserving the cooking water, and blend until smooth. If necessary, thin with a little of the reserved cooking water.

3. Serve lukewarm, or store for up to 48 hours in the refrigerator, or up to 8 weeks in the freezer.

 TIP: It is best to choose a sweet apple for this recipe rather than a tart baking apple, which will be too tart and acidic for delicate stomachs.

9

Peach and Raspberry Puree

Raspberries provide good amounts of vitamin C, which is important for a healthy immune system. Serving foods rich in vitamin C with cereals, such as baby rice cereal, will help your baby to absorb iron.

INGREDIENTS:

2 ripe peaches
¼ cup water
⅔ cup raspberries

PREPARE	COOK	SERVINGS
5 minutes	12-15 minutes	4

1. Score a cross on the bases of the peaches and drop into a bowl of boiling water. Let stand for 1-2 minutes, then drain. Peel off the skins from the peaches, and chop the flesh, removing and discarding the pits. Place the chopped peaches in a small saucepan with the water.

2. Cover and gently cook for 8-10 minutes. Check regularly to make sure the fruit has not caught on the bottom of the saucepan.

3. Add the raspberries and continue cooking for a further 4-5 minutes, until the fruit is soft.

4. Blend until smooth. If desired, press the mixture through a sieve or mouli to remove the raspberry seeds.

5. Serve lukewarm, or store for up to 48 hours in the refrigerator, or up to 8 weeks in the freezer.

Apricot and Banana Baby Rice

Apricots are rich in beta-carotene, which the body can convert into vitamin A. Vitamin A has a number of important functions, such as the development of healthy eyes and skin.

INGREDIENTS:
2 small fresh apricots
2 tablespoons of water
⅓ cup baby rice cereal
½ small ripe banana

PREPARE
5 minutes

COOK
10-12 minutes

SERVINGS
1

1. Score a cross on the bases of the apricots and drop into a bowl of boiling water. Let stand for 1-2 minutes, then drain. Peel off the skins from the apricots and chop the flesh, removing and discarding the pits. Place the chopped apricots in a small saucepan with the water.

2. Cover and simmer gently for 9-10 minutes, until very soft. Check regularly to make sure that the fruit has not caught on the bottom of the saucepan. Let cool a little.

3. Blend until smooth. Stir the baby rice cereal into the apricot.

4. Peel the banana and mash with a fork until smooth, then combine with the apricot and rice mixture.

5. Serve immediately. Do not refrigerate or freeze.

Purple Oatmeal

Oats are a highly nutritious choice at breakfast time (or at any time of the day!) as they release their energy slowly, making little stomachs feel full for longer. Berries are rich in antioxidants.

INGREDIENTS:

½ cup mixed berries, such as raspberries, strawberries, blackberries, and blueberries

3 tablespoons rolled oats

½ cup whole milk

PREPARE
5 minutes

COOK
5 minutes

SERVINGS
1

1. Hull the strawberries, if using, and check over the remaining berries to make sure all the stems have been removed. Blend all the berries until smooth. If desired, press the mixture through a strainer or food mill to remove any seeds or skins. For older babies, you can reserve some of the berries and chop into small chunks to add texture.

2. Put the oats and milk into a small saucepan and bring to a boil. Reduce the heat and simmer gently, stirring occasionally, for 5 minutes, or until thickened. Let cool a little.

3. Pour the oatmeal into a serving bowl and stir in the fruit puree. Scatter over the chopped fruit, if using.

4. Serve lukewarm or store for up to 48 hours in the refrigerator. Do not freeze.

Avocado Puree

The avocado is a rich source of monosaturated fats for heart health and is packed with important nutrients. If your baby is not keen on avocado on its own, try mixing it with banana.

INGREDIENTS:
½ small ripe avocado
dash of whole milk (optional)

PREPARE	COOK	SERVINGS
5 minutes	0 minutes	1

1. Remove the pit from the avocado and scoop out the flesh with a spoon. Mash with a fork until smooth. If desired, mix the avocado with a little milk for a runnier consistency.

2. Serve immediately. Do not refrigerate or freeze.

 TIP: You will need to prepare this puree just before serving because avocado flesh discolors very quickly after it has been cut

Carrot Puree

Root vegetables, such as carrots and sweet potatoes, are ideal as first weaning foods because they are naturally sweet. Carrots contain a good range of vitamins and minerals and help to keep the eyes healthy.

INGREDIENTS:

2 small carrots or
1/2 medium carrot

dash of whole milk
(optional)

PREPARE
5 minutes

COOK
10-15 minutes

SERVINGS
1-2

1. Peel the carrot and cut into 3⅛-inch dice. Steam or cook in enough unsalted boiling water just to cover for about 10-15 minutes, or until soft.

2. Drain the carrot, reserving the cooking water, and blend until smooth. If necessary, thin with a little of the reserved cooking water or some milk, if using.

3. Serve lukewarm, or store for up to 48 hours in the refrigerator, or up to 8 weeks in the freezer.

Green Bean, Zucchini, and Pea Puree

Frozen vegetables can be just as nutritious as fresh ones because they are frozen within hours of being picked. If you wish to use fresh peas for this recipe, add them to the pan along with the beans and zucchini.

INGREDIENTS:

½ cup young green beans

½ small zucchini

3 tablespoons frozen peas

PREPARE
5 minutes

COOK
10 minutes

SERVINGS
2

1. Trim and cut the beans into 1—inch lengths. Trim and roughly chop the zucchini—there is no need to peel it.

2. Steam or cook the beans and zucchini in enough unsalted boiling water just to cover for about 6 minutes. Add the peas and cook for an additional 4 minutes.

3. Drain the vegetables, reserving the cooking water, and blend until smooth. If necessary, thin with a little of the reserved cooking water. If neccessary, press the mixture through a strainer or food mill to remove any stringy parts from the beans and the pea skins.

4. Serve lukewarm, or store for up to 48 hours in the refrigerator, or up to 8 weeks in the freezer.

Popeye's Puree

Although spinach doesn't contain as much iron as once thought, it is still a good source of several other nutrients. These include group B vitamins and vitamin K, which is important for healthy blood and bones.

INGREDIENTS:

2 russet or Yukon gold potatoes

1 McIntosh, Fuji, or Pippin apple

2 cups of fresh spinach

1 cup whole milk

PREPARE
5 minutes

COOK
12-15 minutes

SERVINGS
5-6

1. Peel and cube the potatoes. Peel, core, and dice the apple. Remove any tough stalks from the spinach.

2. Place the potatoes, apple, and milk in a saucepan over a medium heat. Cover and gently simmer for 10-12 minutes, until the potatoes are almost tender.

3. Add the spinach, re-cover, and simmer for a further 2-3 minutes, until it has wilted and the potatoes are tender. Blend until smooth.

4. Serve lukewarm, or store for up to 48 hours in the refrigerator, or up to 8 weeks in the freezer.

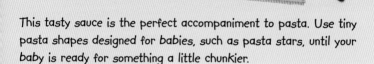

Five-Vegetable Sauce with Pasta

This tasty sauce is the perfect accompaniment to pasta. Use tiny pasta shapes designed for babies, such as pasta stars, until your baby is ready for something a little chunkier.

INGREDIENTS:

1 tablespoon vegetable oil

1 small onion, finely chopped

1 small carrot, peeled and finely chopped

½ red bell pepper, deseeded and finely chopped

1 small zucchini, trimmed and finely chopped

½ cup water

1 cup tomato paste or tomato sauce

2-3 fresh basil leaves, chopped

3 ounces (about ½ cup) baby pasta shapes

PREPARE
10 minutes

COOK
30 minutes

SERVINGS
4-6

1. Heat the oil in a saucepan over a medium heat and cook the onion and carrot for 5 minutes. Add the red bell pepper and zucchini and cook for 1–2 minutes. Add the water, cover, and simmer for 15 minutes. Add the passata and basil and cook until the sauce has reduced and thickened. Blend the sauce to the desired consistency.

2. Meanwhile, cook the pasta according to the packet instructions, until it is tender. Drain and return to the saucepan, then stir in the sauce.

3. Serve lukewarm, or store for up to 48 hours in the refrigerator, or up to 8 weeks in the freezer.

Spring Vegetable Rice

Rice is perfect for babies as the grains are soft, squashy, and easy to eat. This recipe uses spring vegetables, but you can experiment with any others that you have to hand.

INGREDIENTS:

small leek, trimmed and finely chopped

small zucchini, trimmed and finely chopped

small handful of frozen peas

1 teaspoon olive oil

small pat of unsalted butter or polyunsaturated margarine

½ cup risotto rice

1 ½ cups water

½ teaspoon dried oregano

2 tablespoons shredded Cheddar cheese

1. Steam or cook the leek, zucchini, and peas in enough unsalted boiling water just to cover for 5-8 minutes. Drain. If desired, press the mixture through a strainer or food mill to remove the pea skins.

2. Meanwhile, heat the oil and butter in a saucepan until the butter has melted. Add the rice and stir until the grains are coated with the oil and butter.

3. Add the water, a ladleful at a time, waiting until it has been absorbed before adding more. Simmer for 20 minutes, stirring frequently. Add the oregano, cheese and vegetable puree and cook, stirring, for a further 5-10 minutes, until the liquid has been absorbed, and the rice is tender. Blend until smooth, adding a little water if it is too thick. For older babies, you can leave the mixture chunky.

4. Serve lukewarm, or store for up to 48 hours in the refrigerator, or up to 8 weeks in the freezer.

PREPARE
5 minutes

COOK
35-40 minutes

SERVINGS
6-8

Squash and Spinach Puree

Orange-fleshed butternut squash is rich in carotenes and its sweet taste is very appealing to babies. Spinach doesn't contain as much iron as was once thought; nevertheless, it has many health benefits.

INGREDIENTS:

wedge of butternut squash (about ⅛ of the squash)

1 cup fresh spinach leaves

dash of whole milk (optional)

PREPARE
5 minutes

COOK
20 minutes

SERVINGS
2

1. Peel the butternut squash and scoop out the seeds. Cut the flesh into small cubes. Remove any tough stems from the spinach.

2. Steam or cook the squash in enough unsalted boiling water just to cover, for about 15 minutes. Add the spinach and cook for a further 5 minutes.

3. Drain the squash and spinach, reserving the cooking water, and blend until smooth. If necessary, thin with a little of the reserved cooking water or some milk, if using.

4. Serve lukewarm, or store for up to 48 hours in the refrigerator, or up to 8 weeks in the freezer.

Sweet Potato and Pea Puree

Peas are a good source of protein, group B vitamins, vitamin C, and dietary fiber. In addition, the vitamin C from the peas will make it easy for your baby to absorb the iron in the sweet potatoes.

INGREDIENTS:
1 sweet potato
½ cup whole milk
1 cup frozen peas

PREPARE
5 minutes

COOK
12-15 minutes

SERVINGS
2-3

1. Peel the sweet potato and cut into small cubes.

2. Place the sweet potato and milk in a small saucepan over a medium heat. Cover and simmer for 10-12 minutes. Add the peas and continue cooking for a further 2-3 minutes, until soft.

3. Blend until smooth. If desired, press the mixture through a strainer or food mill to remove the pea skins.

4. Serve lukewarm, or store for up to 48 hours in the refrigerator, or up to 8 weeks in the freezer.

Pea and Carrot Puree

The antioxidant beta-carotene gives carrots their characteristic orange color. In the body, beta-carotene can also be converted into vitamin A, which is important for healthy skin and eyes.

INGREDIENTS:

3 carrots

1 cup whole milk

1 1/3 cups frozen peas

PREPARE
5 minutes

COOK
15-20 minutes

SERVINGS
3-4

1. Peel and finely chop the carrots. Place the carrots and milk in a small saucepan over a medium heat. Cover and simmer for 12-15 minutes.

2. Add the peas and cook for a further 2-3 minutes, until everything is soft. Blend until smooth. If desired, press the mixture through a strainer or food mill to remove the pea skins.

3. Serve lukewarm, or store for up to 48 hours in the refrigerator, or up to 8 weeks in the freezer.

Baby's First Beef Stew

Although foods like beans, pulses, and dark green, leafy vegetables contain iron, red meat is a more efficient source of iron as it contains it in a form that is more easily absorbed.

INGREDIENTS:

½ onion. finely chopped

1 garlic clove. crushed

2 large carrots. peeled and chopped

8 ounces of boneless beef chuck or beef round. trimmed of any fat and cubed

2 yukon gold or white round potatoes. peeled and cubed

1 cup water

pinch of dried mixed herbs

PREPARE
10 minutes

COOK
1 ½-2 hours

SERVINGS
5-6

1. Preheat the oven to 325°F. Place all the ingredients in a flameproof casserole dish. Place over a medium heat and bring to a boil, then cover, and transfer to the preheated oven to cook for 1-2 hours, until the vegetables are tender, and the meat starts to fall apart. Blend until smooth.

2. Serve lukewarm, or store for up to 48 hours in the refrigerator, or up to 8 weeks in the freezer.

Beef and Potato Puree

Red meat is an excellent source of iron, which is an important nutrient for babies and toddlers. Babies are born with a store of iron that lasts for about 6 months, but after that they need to have iron in their diet.

INGREDIENTS:

½ red onion, finely chopped

8 ounces boneless beef chuck or beef round, trimmed of any fat and cubed

2 yukon gold or white round potatoes, peeled and cubed

1 cup water

pinch of dried thyme

PREPARE
5 minutes

COOK
1 ½ - 2 hours

SERVINGS
4-5

1. Preheat the oven to 325°F. Place all the ingredients in a flameproof casserole dish. Place over a medium heat and bring to a boil, then cover and transfer to the preheated oven to cook for 1½-2 hours, until the vegetables are tender and the meat starts to fall apart. Blend until smooth.

2. Serve lukewarm, or store for up to 48 hours in the refrigerator, or up to 8 weeks in the freezer.

Chicken, Mushroom, and Apple Mash

Babies can sometimes be put off by the dry texture of chicken, so mixing it with vegetables in a soft puree is a good way of introducing it to your little one's diet. For older babies, you can leave the mixture chunky.

PREPARE
10 minutes

COOK
25 minutes

SERVINGS
2-3

INGREDIENTS:

2 teaspoons of olive oil

1/4 cup finely chopped leek

2 ounces skinless, boneless chicken breast, finely chopped

1/3 cup finely chopped button mushrooms

1/2 potato or 1/4 sweet potato, peeled and diced

1/2 small McIntosh, Fuji, or Pippin apple, peeled, cored, and chopped

2/3 cup water

1. Heat the oil in a small saucepan over a medium heat. Add the leek and chicken and cook, stirring occasionally, for 8–10 minutes, until the leek is tender and the chicken is cooked through, but not browned.

2. Add the mushrooms, potato, and apple. Pour in the water, cover and simmer gently for about 15 minutes, until the vegetables are tender. Blend until smooth.

3. Serve lukewarm, or store for up to 48 hours in the refrigerator, or up to 8 weeks in the freezer.

Thanksgiving Supper

Adding fresh or dried fruit, such as cranberries or dried apricots, to savory dishes helps to boost flavor, interest, and texture. It also provides the antioxidant vitamin C.

INGREDIENTS:

1 large sweet potato, peeled and cubed

6 ounces turkey cutlet, cubed

½ onion, finely chopped

1 ¼ cups water

pinch of dried sage

1 cup short green bean pieces

½ cup fresh cranberries

PREPARE
5 minutes

COOK
20-30 minutes

SERVINGS
6-7

1. Place the sweet potato, turkey, onion, water, and sage in a saucepan over a medium heat. Cover and bring to simmering point, then cook gently for 15-20 minutes.

2. Add the green beans and cranberries and cook for a further 5-10 minutes, until the turkey is thoroughly cooked, and the vegetables are tender. Blend until smooth.

3. Serve lukewarm, or store for up to 48 hours in the refrigerator, or up to 8 weeks in the freezer.

Sweet and Sour Chicken Puree with Noodles

During the weaning process, it is important to introduce your baby to a variety of textures and flavors. Stir-fries are a good way to do this, but don't add soy sauce because it is too salty.

INGREDIENTS:

4 ounces dried fine egg noodles

1 teaspoon vegetable oil

½ onion, finely chopped

½ red bell pepper, seeded and chopped

1 small carrot, peeled and chopped

8 oz skinless, boneless chicken breast, cubed

1 tablespoon tomato paste

½ cup canned pineapple chunks in juice (drained weight), plus 1 cup juice from the can

1. Cook the noodles according to the package instructions. Drain, then cover, and keep warm.

2. Heat the oil in a saucepan over a medium-high heat and cook the onion, red bell pepper, carrot, and chicken for 4–5 minutes, stirring frequently. Add the tomato paste and cook for 1 minute, stirring continuously.

3. Add the pineapple juice, cover, and simmer for 15 minutes. Add the pineapple chunks, replace the lid, and cook for a further 5 minutes, making sure that the chicken is thoroughly cooked.

4. Snip the noodles into short lengths with scissors or chop to a size that is manageable for your baby. Blend the chicken mixture until smooth, then stir in the noodles.

5. Serve lukewarm, or store for up to 48 hours in the refrigerator, or up to 8 weeks in the freezer.

PREPARE
10 minutes

COOK
30–35 minutes

SERVINGS
5–6

Chicken, Mushroom, and Corn Pasta

Chicken is a good source of protein, which is needed for growth and development. It also provides group B vitamins and the mineral zinc, which is important for a healthy immune system.

INGREDIENTS:

1/4 onion, finely chopped

1/3 cup mushrooms, sliced

4 ounces skinless, boneless chicken breast, cubed

1/4 cup corn kernels, canned in water and drained, or frozen

1/2 cup whole milk

1 ounce (about 3 tablespoons) baby pasta shapes

PREPARE
5 mins

COOK
20-25 minutes

SERVINGS
2

1. Place all the ingredients, except the pasta, in a saucepan. Cover and simmer gently for 15 minutes, stirring occasionally, until the chicken is thoroughly cooked. Blend until smooth. If wished, press the mixture through a strainer or food mill to remove the corn skins.

2. Meanwhile, cook the pasta according to the packet instructions until it is tender. Drain well. Stir the pasta into the chicken puree.

3. Serve lukewarm or store for up to 48 hours in the refrigerator. Do not freeze.

contents:

date made:

contents:

date made:

contents:

date made:

contents:

date made:

contents:

date made:

contents:

date made:

Creamy Turkey Puree with Pasta

Turkey is a good source of lean protein, as well as the group B vitamins, niacin and B6, which are needed for a healthy nervous system. It also provides phosphorous, which is important for strong bones.

PREPARE
5 minutes

COOK
20-25 minutes

SERVINGS
5-6

INGREDIENTS:

1 teaspoon vegetable oil

¼ onion, finely chopped

2 small carrots, peeled and chopped

6 ounces turkey cutlet, cubed

1 cup whole milk

¾ cup short green bean pieces

2 ounces (about ⅓ cup) baby pasta shapes

1. Heat the oil in a saucepan and cook the onion and carrot for 2-3 minutes, until softened. Add the turkey and milk, then bring to simmering point. Cover and cook gently for 10-12 minutes.

2. Add the green beans and cook for a further 2-3 minutes, until the turkey is thoroughly cooked, and the vegetables are tender.

3. Meanwhile, cook the pasta according to the package instructions until it is tender. Drain well. Blend the turkey mixture until smooth, then stir in the pasta.

4. Serve lukewarm, or store for up to 48 hours in the refrigerator, or up to 8 weeks in the freezer.

31

Index